EARNING MORE MONEY THROUGH SECOND INCOME, WHILE DEALING WITH CHANGE

RECOGNIZING YOUR NEED FOR A SECOND INCOME WHILE PREPARING YOURSELF FOR CHANGE

Copyright © 2018. All Rights Reserved.

No part of this publication may be reproduced, distributed, or transmitted in any form or by any means, including photocopying, recording, or other electronic or mechanical methods, or by any information storage and retrieval system without the prior written permission of the publisher, except in the case of very brief quotations embodied in critical reviews and certain other noncommercial uses permitted by copyright law.

Why You Should Read This Book

This book will enlighten you on the need for a second income, while preparing you for for change or overcoming change. There by providing you the right guardian to overcome any financial problems. Consequently improviing your overall well being while living a beta life...

Table of Contents

Why You Should Read This Book

Table of Contents

Chapter 1. introduction

Chapter 2. Why do you need a second income source

Chapter 3. Who am I?

Chapter 4. Understand my language

Chapter 5. Thing to look out for in a good side hustle

Chapter 7. Characteristics of a great side hustle

Chapter 8. The basics

Chapter 9. "Barriers" to change

Chapter 10. A summary stories on few People

chapter 11. conclusion

Am sure we are all aware of the current economic situation we are facing around the world, this is one of the major reason why we always struggle to make all necessary preparation. We struggle to save the little we earn, we always find a way to maximize the cash we have at hand. Struggle is good. Struggle is necessary, as we all know It creates resolve and respect for money, however it not the best we can do.

We need to know just how to earn more money, while dealing with changes; changes in the economy, changes at work, changes in your family and household issues.

Are you middle class worker, are you the 8 to 8 type, are you still wondering when you will be promoted in other to get an increase in your salary. All this are known as a primary income, with a primary income in the current situation of the economy you can't really go far.

Come to think of your daily expense, weekly expense and monthly expense, take a pen and put down your daily, weekly and monthly expense add them all together and deduct it from your salary you hardly get to save a cent and that's if you don't have to get a credit card to pass the month.

A lot of people in the U.S live on debt, they live all their lives from one credit to the other which is not supposed to be so.

You need to recognize your need for a second income, come to think of it you don't always have to live your life in debt when you have an option to go for, what is the option you have? You need a second income source.

Are you sick of toiling and working your hands to the bone but it's never enough? Most likely you have already researched opportunities to earn more money so you can support your household but came up short. Feel misled? I understand! In these trying times, one income can barely sustain living requirements, never mind handle an entire family. Additionally, spouses are forced to look for "sub-par" jobs to hopefully make ends meet while many are sacrificing quality time with their families. Does this sound like an ideal environment?

What are your goals for your second income? The answer to this question is very important because it will identify which opportunities you should research. Are you looking for an extra few hundred dollars or do you desire to begin a path to complete financial freedom? If you just need some extra money, you can research the restaurants, shops and stores in your neighborhood that are looking for part-time employees. If you are a mother who loves kids, you could start a daycare in your home or help other mothers drive their kids to school or after school activities. If you are interested in dogs, why not help the neighborhood by walking dogs to make a few extra bucks.

Most of the people I mentor desire a second income not only to pay their bills, but also to eventually rid their lives of debt and begin a lifestyle of financial freedom. They are sick of the professional daily grind, corporate nonsense and unending financial stress! They are determined to make a change. They want freedom from worrying about where their next paycheck is coming from. They long for the finer things in life such as more time with their loved ones and freedom to make decisions based on their desires not the state of their wallets. The best business ideas to approach this lifestyle arise from the internet.

If you are tired of the endless struggle, you need to start planning now to find a home based internet opportunity that will change your life and give you the ability to make a substantial second income. You deserve another chance and an opportunity to slam the door in the face of your financial worries! You can work as little or as hard as you want depending on how much money you desire to make. It definitely will require a commitment, but your financial state is unique to you and how you handle it is your prerogative.

Why do you need a second income source

We all have goals, don't we? If you don't, then I am not sure what to say to you. Step away from this post and go write down something you want to achieve.

Ok, now for those that have goals. Let's talk about how you plan on achieving them. John and I both are advocates of setting goals.They are extremely important and help you understand where you are and were you want to go.Without them, it can be very hard to achieve much.

A GOAL THAT REQUIRES EXTRA INCOME

One of my main goals this year is to sell our current home and then buy another one. Now, selling and buying a home is a hectic process as all homeowners know. The entire process is time consuming and it costs a lot of money. I have been saving as much money as I can with each paycheck, but after some time, I realized that I wasn't saving enough.

There are two ways to deal with this problem. I could cut services that I pay for on a monthly basis, or I could earn more. You can only cut expenses by so much before you are going to hit a wall. Unfortunately for me, I have hit that wall. So, my best option was to make more money.

I can't go to my boss and ask for a raise, as we only get annual reviews, so that would be a waste of time. What I can do is look for income producing opportunities on the side. It has been about seven months since I have ramped up my efforts to earn extra income and I can say that I have reached my goal. I now have enough money in my savings account to be comfortable when paying a down payment and having an emergency fund. This wouldn't have been possible without earning extra income.

Earn extra income

The primary reason most people get a second job is to earn extra income, whether it's to pay off debt, cover vacation or seasonal expenses, or add to their current income. "We hear frequently from job seekers that they take a second job with a specific purchase in mind," Parker says.

However, for many others, taking the second job will mean making the mortgage payment that month. A study in August by Chicago-based CareerBuilder.com found 42 percent of full-time workers usually or always live paycheck to paycheck just to make ends meet. "A steady job often isn't enough to get by, prompting people to find additional work,"

Lower risk of primary job loss

Let's face it; the job market is less than stellar these days, and workers have a real fear of losing their jobs, especially since many full-time employees are living paycheck to paycheck. To mitigate that risk, people are taking second jobs.

"A lot of workers are still leery about job security, making a second job a popular safety net," says Hunt. "However, workers who take this path need to make sure their performance doesn't deteriorate due to the increased workload."

According to Parker, taking a second job especially makes sense if layoffs are happening or the future of the primary employer is in doubt. It will not only increase your nest egg, but it may be a way to get in the door at a company since many employers look for workers who are willing to move from part-time to full-time employees, Parker says. He also points out that most states will let you work part-time and still collect some unemployment benefits.

Not working in fear

Majority of all primary workers work in fear on daily basics, fear of intimidation from superior, fear of work place gossips, and mostly the fear surrounding an unsavory workplace culture.

We need to stop working in fear, fear leads to anxiety and so many health problems, so in other to defeat this fear you need a second income source.

There are so many benefits you will get if you stop working in fear, like health benefits, social benefits , personal benefits and much more. When you stop working in fear you gain peace and happiness while working which indirectly improve your working performance, social reasons; you tends to engage with people in the society, new members in the community and you have the potentials of making new friends.

Indirectly you tend to increase a network within which to prospect and mine for new side hustle opportunities.

Personal development reasons; Creating a new income stream is a psychological challenge. Overcoming something that you thought was once impossible, it gives you a sense of victory, a sense of confidence and purpose, you gain inner peace and let not forget that indirectly you are acquiring a new skill, new business skill or ideal and most of all you tend to achieve an 100% job satisfaction.

It help to transition out of one primary income stream to another

64% of Americans are working in a department or industry they are not passionate about, they are committed to a work culture they don't agree with, all because they had to make money thay had to suvive. Having a second income can make you realize your passion and if you work towards it you will defiantly be able to transition out of the primary income stream you are not passionate about into what you are passionate about whereby making it your primary income. You don't have to always trade your time and health for too little in return.

Who am I?

I am the product of repeated failure. This has created a survivor who is now a thriver. By failing repeatedly, I have learnt resilience but also the importance of a second income stream and the flexibility and security it provides.

I can show you what has worked for me in exchange for some time credits

The presidential election is over and I can tell you now. President Donald Trump is not going to save you. You are going to need more income. Senator Hillary Clinton couldn't save your finances, either. The truth is the middle class is dead. That dream of finding a good job, buying a house, having a car, and saving to retire to greener pastures is an illusion.

Don't believe me. Look at all the fast food jobs, security, and customer service jobs out there. There is not a job shortage. Jobs are everywhere if you are willing to work for minimum wage or a little higher. The unemployment rate has gone down every year since the last recession. Americans are scared because they are living paycheck to paycheck. They are in debt up to their eyeballs. One setback and they can be financially ruined.

Don't think the middle class is dead. Will the next POTUS bring back a resurgence of the middle class? Heck no, it has been in decline for over 30 years. Think about it. If you are making $100k in places like Los Angeles, New York, San Francisco or Chicago you are struggling. Especially, if you are carrying student loans, a mortgage, and huge credit card debts.

The Journey of The Broke

Go to work, get paid, and then barley make it to the next paycheck. Then use credit cards, pay-day loans, or home equity lines to bridge the gap until you get paid again. That is the journey of the broke. A vicious cycle that hits most American homes today. People are not getting ahead. You can blame the economy, greedy corporations, or bad trade deals. Ultimately why you are broke is because of YOU.

Until you create more income the cycle of debt and not enough money will repeat itself. Income is king to financial security. This is where people fail. They do not create more income. Sure cutting expenses and having a monthly cashflow plan can help your finances. But until you increase that income line... you will struggle.

Understand my language

Enjoyment of life: This is the ultimate goal. The enjoyment of life from my perspective is repeated moments of happiness, all you need to do is to follow my lead to living a life of enjoyment

Time: time is a limited resource and it is a limited resource to all people.... nobody is living forever. People who work to finance their existence sell their time in return for money. This is common to all people who work for a living. We sell our time to an employer who utilizes our particular skillset. The skillset we have can be upgraded and it can also degrade over time and become less valuable to the marketplace.

Health: health is a fundamental ingredient to the enjoyment of life. Itis also a resource and whilst our bodies can heal and renew it degrades over time. When we sell time to an employer we are also trading in a component of health. Some occupations take a physical toll on our bodies more than others and other occupations take a heavier mental toll on our mental wellbeing.

Money: money is just time credits. You need to understand that money is a time credit as I said above, It is a store of time value.

Making Time: This has two meaning. First we can make time by being more efficient in how we do things. Simply by completing two tasks in a one hour time slot that previously took two hours to complete creates one hour of time. Creating time in this manner is all about the old adage of working smarter and not harder. Mothers who run a busy household are really good at this! The second meaning is about forward planning. Its when you block out time in the diary for yourself. It could be for any activity that you enjoy, that rejuvenates your health or give you some particular enjoyment of life. Making time for yourself in this way is also very important.

Buying time: Simply having enough money to own your time rather than being in a constant cycle of selling time to others with very little left for yourself. The real crux is to be in a position where you own your own time with enough health to have an abundance of repeated moments of happiness. In other words a great retirement!

Your price: How much do you earn an hour in your primary income? You must know this because this is the key measurement to allocating your time properly. A second income stream must earn more on an hourly basis than your primary income stream... otherwise you are better off spending more time at your primary workplace.

As workers we have transitioned from being farm workers to urban workers.

To work land for survival requires a broad range of skills and a broad range of knowledge that is generally rewarded with low levels of income.

An urban worker has a narrower more specialized range of skills and range of knowledge. The advantages of this is higher levels of income, more leisure time and historically a higher standard of living. A significate disadvantage of this transition is that the primary income stream is perhaps riskier. Urban jobsare more exposed to changes in local demand and supply. Urban jobs can be sent offshore to a country with cheaper urban workers. And increasingly urban jobs are under threat from computers.

An urban worker has a lot of money outflows. Urban workers have a lot of expected money outflows like rent, vehicle registrations, rates, bank fees etc. And urban workers have lots of unexpected money outflows. For example, parking fines, constant replacing of expensive sunglasses, constant replacing of smart phones, constant upgrades of electrical household goods and medical bills. Urban workers also outsource a lot of services. For example, cleaning, building repairs, motor vehicle maintenance and cooking.

It is the outsourcing of services that provides the opportunity to create a second income stream.

Thing to look out for in a good side hustle

Legal

False premise: illegal activities produce easy money.

1. Illegal activities require equal amounts of hard work and organisation as legal activities.

2. You have to service clients outside of business hours.

3. You deal with unsavoury characters; slowly their values become interwoven into your own and its hard to unravel them.

4. Large amounts of cash creates problems. Your time credits can be easily stolen and are ineffective in building wealth hidden under the bed.

5. You are exposed to violence and intimidation.

6. Risk incarceration and significant losses of time.

Low barriers to entry

High barriers to entry drain resources. The key objective is to get cash in quickly. Although once you are operating high barriers to entry are your friend.

Quick to learn

The key objective is to get cash in quickly. Long courses drain resources.

Paid in cash

There is no credit risk in a cash transaction. This saves on time because there is zero chance of needing to chase up payment. Don't underestimate the stress of chasing up people for money owed. There is no bigger waste of time.

You also have control of the tax you pay. Pay as little as you can because the government is willing to take as much as possible – fairness may be found in the middle ground.

Higher rate of return than primary income

Workers sell their time. If your primary income makes $30/hr and your side hustle makes you $20/hr then just work an extra shift at your primary job. However, tax needs to be considered because your side hustle may be tax free which will even things out. And the fact that rapid change could occur and you could loose your primary. It would be fantastic in that situation to have a secondary income stream that could be boosted by the extra time you will now have…..

Ideally though you want the second income stream to be much more lucrative than your primary income stream on an hourly basis….

Characteristics of a great side hustle

Upscale

Who wouldn't want more of a good thing. If it pays well and you enjoy it then it may be worth considering turning it in to your primary income stream.

Upsale

Your clients will have different budgets. You need to maximise your rate of return by having the ability to upsale. Have a budget option and a luxury option and price them accordingly. More service, more margin and more money in.

Repeat customers

When you have customers that come back regularly it saves you time and money in advertising. Treat them well but do not be taken advantage of by them. Your time is still precious even if you are not busy.

Where to find side hustles

Look around at the successful services in your area. Some successful side hustles will already have evolved into larger business. They will now have higher running costs and be charging their clients more for the same service. You could identify them, learn the craft and price match them for a handsome return because of your lower running costs.

Listen out for your friends and family complain about a service that was expensive and left them feeling unsatisfied. No doubt there will be more people who feel the same way about that service provider. Figure out how to learn the skill, what the set-up costs are, what are the input costs and what the likely hourly rate of return for your time is. If you can get to that point then you are almost there.

Always be on the lookout for side hustles.

The basics

These four things are what most of us need to get started. They are barriers to entry but there will be some people out there who don't need these to start a good hustle.

1. Primary job: This gives you a means to survive.

2. Stable home base: In order to connect into a community and start a service hustle you must be established in that area.

3. Home office: This is a hidden start up cost and it can be substantial. It involves a computer, printer/scanner, word processing software, spreadsheet software, computer virus protection etc

4. Smartphone

What if you don't have the basics

1. Work towards getting the basics. OR

2. Find a completely mobile side hustle and use a smart phone.

Other bits of advice

1. Show negative people the exit way, identify negative people in you life and showing them the exit way, you cant go far when you always have to watch your back for negative people. Kindly identify them and show them the way out of your life.

2. Taking care of your body: always take good care of your body, eat well, exercise regularly because exercise is one of the key to healthy living, and tell funny stories or jokes regularly. eat good food with friends and loved ones as often as possible.

"Barriers" to change

When you decide to make significant positive change in your life, it can be a bit scary. Depending on where you are starting from, you could end up becoming a whole different person-a person you never dreamed you could be. Adopting a whole new set of beliefs, habits and actions has lots of implications that can serve as barriers to this transformation and keep you stuck where you are. One of the biggest barriers is other people. You need courage to overcome them so you can continue your transition to the best you possible. You need to realize that you are embarking on a journey that few attempt-let alone even consider.

One of the biggest fears we have about significant change is the worry about how other people will perceive us. We care so much about what other people think and we dread being the topic of gossip, scorn or criticism. Bold change calls attention to us. The people around us begin to notice the differences. They might not understand. They might not agree. They might be jealous. They might think you are weird. They might be angry that the new you no longer serves their needs or interferes with what they want. If you want to achieve true happiness and live an authentic life being who you really are, you need to accept that most people around you are not striving for these same things-they might want to but might not believe they can or they are so ingrained in negative habitual thought patterns that they are not even aware of their capacity for change. As long as people continue to be unhappy with their own lives, they will always gossip and judge-and none of us are immune from the judgment of others so you need to learn to accept that this judgment will fly your way on occasion.

Another impediment to significant positive change is worrying about the impact it will have on your relationships. Deep inner work inevitably requires you to evaluate everything in your life- including your relationships. As you continue on your journey, you might find that you are no longer compatible with the people around you as you are no longer the same person you were when the relationships started. I am not saying to dump everyone who does not share your outlooks and beliefs but you might find that as you interests and goals change, the foundations that sustained certain relationships begin to crumble away. If you commit to becoming a more positive person, it might be hard to sustain relationships with people who are predominantly negative. If you develop a passion for exploring the mysteries of the universe and personal development, it might be hard to spend all of your time with people who do nothing but watch reality TV all day long. You might come to some sad realizations. For example, you might think you have a close relationship with someone but realize it is only held together by a shared love of something that you have come to realize is destructive for you-like drugs or getting black-out drunk every weekend. Once you remove this element, you realize that there is nothing else there. You might be scared if you change too much, you might have to face some deep down fears like admitting you are in a romantic relationship that is not working and probably never will. It can be scary to move away from people you have known your whole life but it might be necessary in some cases.

Sadly, most of us will continue to live on the surface most of our lives. If you decide to transcend this, you will most likely be the odd one out and you need to stay true to yourself and your journey. As you move on, you will find people who share your outlooks and beliefs and you will not be alone. You might find yourself moving away from some of the people in your life now. Do not judge them for not sharing your enthusiasm for living life to the fullest and transcending the fog that most of us live in.Most of us fear going that deep. Everyone has their own path; stay true to yours no matter what happens around you.

A summary stories on few People

These people are all nice people with kind hearts. They all have only ever had one primary income. Only the younger two have time to change. For the most part the future is bleak for the others. They have not prepared for rapid change and/or have not responded well to it.

A Man named dan, in is late 50's; all through his life he worked a safe job in a bank. He is now battling with cancer, he earn an average income his whole life, up till now even on the face of death he cant afford to stop working, he's working just so he can die.

Here is another individual named brian, he is in his early 40's he has work on many various jobs but currently in a 9-5 office job, he had a wife and two young children.

He is on a current bank morgage larger than the value of his home still strugling to pay his household bills. He only goes to a social events that have free alcohol, he cant aford to make any substantial changes in his life. Feels trapped isnt it.

Here is a depressed Teenager, currently an apprentice on a minimum wage, regularly abused by his boss. His boss always tell him that he's useless, why isn't he trying, a shit apprentice. He has no social life, he only plays video games, eat cheap foods, buy low quality goods and surprisingly drinks a whole bottle of bourbon in one sitting.

A Young Tradesman in his late 30's, he is previously a very high income earner in the time of boom economy, now struggling to find work, he can't understand why thing has changed so much for him

Conclusion

Always remember that change is constant, rapid change with extreme outcomes is a possibility and it doesn't matter…. we are all going to be dead one day.

Invest in yourself because the time is always ticking and don't forget the main point of this book "earning more money while dealing with change".

Disclaimer

The information contained within this eBook is strictly for educational purposes. If you wish to apply ideas contained in this eBook, you are taking full responsibility for your actions.

The methods describe within this eBook are the author's personal thoughts. They are not intended to be a definitive set of instructions for this project. You may discover there are other methods and materials to accomplish the same end result.

(self-help, sucess)

ABOUT THE AUTHOR

My name is MARY DAVENPORT, I am the founder and owner of THE ACT OF CREATIVITY (TAOC).

I am first and foremost a mother of 3, grandmother of 8. Have been freelancing for many years now , as a writer before I setup my own organization, i am also currently an hotel general manager and an avid reader..my favorite is kindle publishing though..lol I really love educating people on how to become successful in life, stay healthy and live the life of their dreams

Do not go yet; One last thing to do

If you enjoyed this book or found it useful I'd be very grateful if you'd post a short review on it. Your support really does make a difference and I read all the reviews personally so I can get your feedback and make this book even better.

Thanks again for your support!